Are You Confused and Searching

for the Right Direction?

# THE PATH TO
# RIGHTEOUSNESS?

"GOD IS ABLE" is a provocative self-assessment
of how one should accept God into their livees so that they
could be guided down the path that was intended.

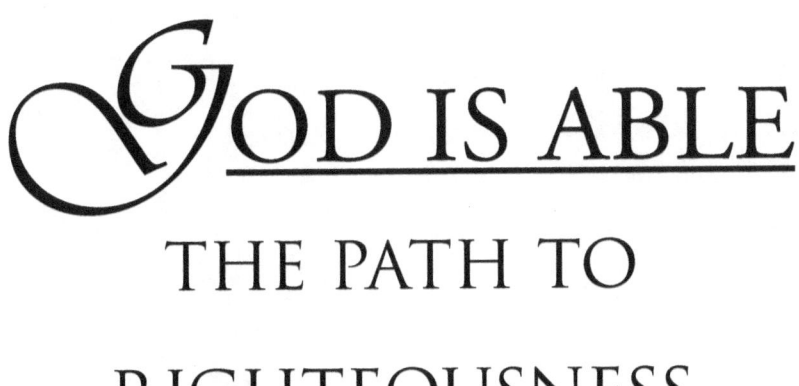

# GOD IS ABLE

## THE PATH TO

## RIGHTEOUSNESS

by

Ms. Bobbie Dorsey Young

authorHOUSE®

AuthorHouse™
1663 Liberty Drive, Suite 200
Bloomington, IN 47403
www.authorhouse.com
Phone: 1-800-839-8640

First published by AuthorHouse     6/23/2009

ISBN: 978-1-4343-9632-7 (sc)

Printed in the United States of America
Bloomington, Indiana

This book is printed on acid-free paper.

# CONTENTS

# MY TESTAMONY

When I was growing up I was a very restless child. I couldn't wait until I finish high school so I could leave home. My father was a Preacher and a very nice man. My mother was a housewife, she was a nice person but we couldn't get along. I couldn't do anything right in her eyesight. I got beaten for things I didn't do and for things I didn't deserve to be beaten for. I try to buy my mother's love because I thought she didn't love me. As a child, I thought

*"If you love someone you won't beat them they way I got beaten."*

I had lots of headaches as a child. I was afraid to express

myself to my mother, so I did a lot of crying. I felt like I had split personality. My parents took me to lots of Doctors but they couldn't find anything wrong with me. They took me to many tent meetings to see if I could be healed. Nothing work. I kept on having headaches. I kept on hoping and dreaming for the day I graduate from school and leave home, because I was so tired of getting beaten with an extension code, stick, knife, or anything she got her hands on. It really hurt me physically and mentally because my brother and I was the only one she beat like that. I had six sisters and six brothers so I couldn't understand why I was getting beat on all the time.

The day of my graduation was a great day for me; I know it won't be long before I could leave home. A month after graduation I went to New York to my oldest sister. I got a job working at the Telephone Company. Every week I would send money home to my mother because I was still trying to buy her love, but it still didn't work. Every time I went home to visit my mother and I would always start auguring and I end up leaving before my vacation is up.

I started having dreams about my mother and every time in my dreams she would make me cry. Sometimes I would wake up out of my sleep crying.

A year and a half after I move to New York I got married. I thought he was a wonderful man until he started beaten on me also. After I had my second child he changed over night. He started drinking alcohol and coming home drunk, which ended up in a fight between us. I felt like a punching bag. I wanted to leave him but my mother told me to stay because of the children. After my third child, which was ten years later I couldn't take it any longer. One day he came home drunk we started fighting, he pick up a recliner and threw it at me that recliner miss me by two inches. So he decided to take his hard sole shoe and hit me on my ankle. My ankle became bruise. The next day I file for a divorce. A few months later I start having problems with my ankle. I went to the Doctor and I found out that the bruise on my ankle turned into a tumor. I had to have an operation on my ankle. The Doctor had to take a bone from my right hip and put it in my ankle because the bones in my ankle were deteriorated. I had to wear a cast for eight month. I had to learn how to walk again. Only three good things came out of my marriage and that was my three lovely children, two boys and one girl.

A few months later I went to a club with friends and I met a man who was playing in the band. I look at him and he look at me and I said, I am not going to leave this club until I talk to him, which I did. We started dating. Things were going great and we started living together. A year later he decided to become a police officer. After three years together I had my daughter. I also found out he had two other children with two other women. I was so angry with him I told him to get out. After he left I called the police station and curse the police department out. Who ever answer the phone I would curse them out and I threaten to bomb the station up. The police trace the call to my house and a few minutes' later three police came to my house and ask me about the threat. I denial everything then I told the police to get out of my house before I call a real police on them. I didn't care any more. I started thinking all men are dogs. I was also so tired with my life the way things were going, one disappointment after another; I thought no one really loved me. So I start hurting people before they got the chance to hurt me. I just didn't care any more. I start dating all kinds of men, from a pimp to a Pastor. If they had money and a car I would date them. No money and no car, No date. I would hurt them before they could hurt me. I would love them and leave them. I dated over fifty men by the time I was forty-seven. All I wanted to do was hurt and use them because I was hurting inside for love. Guess what, while I was hurting them I was also hurting myself because I always felt empty, unloved, and lonely in the end. I was searching for someone to love me but no one did. I didn't trust any one because I was afraid they would hurt me. I started stealing, gambling, and drinking wine. I had no fear of any body and I didn't have any fear of nothing. I felt powerful. The devil really had me and I didn't care at the time because I had no feelings. I dated a hit man, if I wanted some one eliminated all I had to do was tell my man, but I never had to have any one eliminated. One day when I was in his apartment a group of men came running into his apartment and he ran out the back door, I got scared and I call a cab and went home. I dated him for five month and he had to leave town in a hurry and I haven't heard from him again, but before he left town he gave his sister a lot of money to give to me. I didn't know if the money was stolen or what kind of money it was, all I know is that I spend it. After that I start dating a pimp. At the time I start dating him I didn't know he was a pimp. A few weeks after we dated he asks me to prostitute for him. I looked at him and ask him if he was crazy. And I told him, if I ever decide to sell my body it won't be for a man it would be for me because if I am going to get money for selling my body I am going to keep the money and no man was going to get it. So I stop seeing him. After that I dated lots of other men when I got tired of one I would go to another. I couldn't find any one to satisfy me. After that I dated a bank manager. I was moving up in the world. I move from a hit man to a banker. He was married with three children but I didn't care. It was all about me and as long as I got what I wanted that's all that matters. I was no longer working at the telephone company I had a job at the bank and we worked at the same bank. He worked in a different department than I did. We met in the cafeteria. He took me on trips out of town. We stayed in the best hotels because I won't settle for any thing less. He wanted to divorce his wife for me, which he did months later. After that I didn't want him any more. Dating him was getting boring, so I start dating his best friend. We dated for a few months then I start dating the bank manager again. We dated a few more months than I started modeling lingerie part-time for ebony magazine. I also started dating the manager of the modeling agency. A few months after I start working for him he started making movies of me without me knowing about it. I was in his office one day when he was not there and I found out about it. When he came to his office I ask him about it and we got into a fight. I curse him out and I destroy his office and destroy tapes and magazines that was in the office. He start to call the police and I told him to go ahead because I didn't care and I told him I will call my hit man and he will eliminated you, so he didn't call the police again. He told me to get out of his office and I did. He didn't know that the hit man wasn't in town. A few months later I found out some one killed him for making movies of other woman. I stop modeling but I was still working at the bank. I got another part-time job working in a super market. The manager was a handsome man and we started dating. I was still dating the bank manager also. The manager at the super market found out I was also dating one of my customers, so he fired me and wouldn't give me my last check. I had to take the bank manager with me to get my check. A month later I got a part-time job working at another super market. I didn't date any one in this super market. I also got another job working in another bank, which was closer to my apartment. I started dating the manager at this bank also. He was a Spanish guy.

We dated for six months then he embezzles over a million dollars from the bank. The president of the bank found out about it and the manager left town and he didn't even told me he was leaving because the police was looking for him. The police thought I had something to do with it, but I didn't have any thing to do with it. The police gave me a lie detective test. I pass the test. A few months later I heard that the police found him and I really don't know what happen to him after that. The bank hired another manager and I started dating him. He was an Indian. He lived in New Jersey. On weekends I would stay with him in New Jersey. We dated for a few months and I started dating a man from Jamaica. He was an older man and he knew how to cook some good West Indian food. He wanted to take me to Jamaica with him but I was afraid to go because he was too possessive and I was afraid he might do something to me in Jamaica to make me stay with him. He would buy me any thing I wanted only one thing about him that I didn't like was, he was too possessive, so, I stop seeing him because no one owns me.

I guess you are wondering where are my four children all this time. I had a baby sister to keep my two daughters, my two sons were teenagers so they didn't need a baby sitter. After I stop seeing the Jamaica man I started dating a man from a club I hang out to. He was the owner of the club. When I was in the club I would dance if no body else dance. When I see a man that I wanted to dance with I would go to him and start dancing in front of him, I would give him a lap dance and I didn't care if his wife or girlfriend was with him. It was all about me and what I wanted. The women would get mad with me. Some wanted to fight me but I didn't care. Sometimes a man would come to the club with his woman but he would leave with me. My friend at the club didn't like that so we stop dating.

I was still having those terrible headaches. I was still having dreams about my mother and she was still making me cry in my dreams. My father died when I was twenty-seven and my mother died when I was thirty-three. I end up going to a therapist. I had so much on my mind. My mother died before she could love me. I thought she hated me. I started having lots of headaches, so I start seeing a therapist once a week. The therapist told me to write a letter to my mother telling her everything I was afraid to tell her while she was living. I thought that was crazy because she wouldn't be able to read it, but it wrote the letter. When I got through writing the letter to my mother I had a ten- page letter. The next week I took the letter to the therapist and she told me to read the letter out loud just like I was talking to my mother. So I start reading the letter, by the time I got to the third page I started crying, the therapist had tears in her eyes, when I got through reading the letter I felt so much better. The therapist explains to me why my mother treated me the way she did. I understood but I couldn't forget or forgive because I still had a little hurt in my heart.

I still dated lots of men and I still had headaches not as much but I still had them. When I was forty I had another dream about my mother, but this time she told me to leave New York and move back to South Carolina before something bad happens to me. I was doing all kinds of bad things and hanging out with all kinds of bad people when I was in New York, but every Sunday I would go to church because I grew up in church. I would party all week and praise God on Sunday. I kept having that same dream for a year. So I decided to move back to South Carolina. I didn't have enough money to move, so I stole money from the bank. After I got to my apartment and look at the money I got scared so I decided to return the money the next day.

I was a supervisor at the bank so I fix the computer so it will prove out that night. The next day I tried to put the money back in the computer and I got caught. The manager called me into her office and asks me what was I doing? I was so scare so I told her the truth. She called the FBI. I didn't go to jail because I put all the money back. I was asked to resign so I resign and I start working full time at my part-time job. I had to report to the FBI office once a month for a year. I had to stay out of trouble during this time. Two month later I moved to South Carolina. I told the FBI that

I was moving; he got in touch with the FBI in Florence, I had to start going to the FBI's office in Florence. After I got to South Carolina I met a guy at the grocery store and we start talking. He asks me to go to the movie with him and I did. We dated for a month and I told him about the FBI situation because I needed a ride to Florence because I was staying in Georgetown at the time. I also told one of my sisters because I needed a ride from her also. I start dating lots of men again. I just couldn't find what I wanted. This time I was dating Preachers and Pastors and also drug dealers and other guys. Some were married and some wasn't. I really didn't care because it was all about me. I would visit their church and sit right next to their wives and the wives didn't know who I was. While these Pastors were preaching all I could think about is,

> *"They can't tell me a thing because they are cheating on their wives and they were out with me last night or a couple of nights before."*

I knew they weren't a Christian because they were cheating on their wives. I wasn't saved so I didn't care. One pastor I use to date asks me to be his mistress. He told me he would buy me a car, a house, take care of my two daughters and that I wouldn't have to work. I told him no because I didn't want to be kept. No one owns me. Every time there was a Church Conference I was there seeking to see who I could pick up and believe me there was a lot of married Preachers and Pastors waiting to be picked up. Some would leave the church with me and take me out to eat and buy clothes for me and after that we would go to a hotel between services. Some left the wives at church and most of them didn't bring their wives with them to church.

I dated Preachers and Pastors for several years, when I was forty-seven years old I was getting tired of doing the same thing over and over and I still haven't found what I was looking for, I still was lonely and unloved and empty inside so I asked the Lord to forgive me and help me and give me the strength to stop doing what I was doing because I was hurting people and myself. I asked the Lord to have mercy on me and help me to become one of His children. And He did it. He saved me. After I gave my life to Christ I realized that He was with me all the time. If He hadn't been with me I could have been dead, or in jail, or had some kind of disease, but His mercy and grace kept me. I now realized that he is the answer for me. He showed me a new life. He is everything to me. I know without a shadow of doubt that he loves me. When my mother and my family forsaken me He was there for me. He never left me nor forsaken me. I don't have to go looking for love in all the wrong places or in all the wrong men. God loves me because he gave His only begotten son, Jesus, who died on the cross for my sins and rose the third day that I might have the right to the tree of life. He brought me through this and he brought me through that. He delivered me from hatred, fornication, envy, revenge, gambling, stealing, adultery and taught me how to love myself and other people and how to forgive. I didn't really forgave my mother until I got Christ in my life. Jesus gave me love, peace, joy, and happiness. He is my all and all. H e also gave me four lovely children and six lovely grandchildren. I am a new person in Christ. He did it for me and he will do it for you. So if you are running from man to man, you don't have to do it. Run to the only man who can help you and his name is Jesus.

On March 14, 2005, I enter Carolinas hospital system emergency room because I was throwing up. By the time I got there I smelled like vomit and urine because I couldn't stop vomiting and I couldn't hold my urine. My heart was beating irregular, my pressure was high this minute and low the next, and my blood sugar was very high. The Doctors didn't know what was wrong with me, they thought I had a stroke or a heart attack so they put me in the ICU. I started crying because I knew something was very seriously wrong with me. All I could do was pray. My daughter was scared she didn't know what to do and didn't know what was going on. When I got to the intensive care unit and saw all those sick people I started crying even more. Ten minutes after I got to the ICU a patient died. I really got scared then. I started crying and praying, asking the Lord, *"what's wrong with me and please don't let me die."*

I was so scared. I didn't want to be in ICU. The nurses hook me up to all kinds of machines and I was taking all kinds of pills. The next day the doctors gave me all kind of tests. Most of the time I was so weak and dizzy I couldn't remember who came to see me. I didn't have a telephone in my room I couldn't talk to no one. I couldn't hold my urine and bowels, the nurse had to wash and clean me. I was so embarrass.

After being in the ICU for two weeks the Doctors found out that I have a massive tumor on my right adrenal glands right over my right kidneys. When the doctor told me that I was shock, scared, nervous, confuse, and angry. Then the doctor told me it has to come out and it was too big for laser surgery and that I have to be cut. He also told me my adrenal glands would have to come out because the tumor was on it and that he didn't know if my kidneys would have to come out. This was too much for me to handle. All kinds of things ran through my mind. I couldn't understand why this was happening to me. I started crying again so the doctor told me he would give me a few moments to my self so everything could sink in. I cried and I cried until I couldn't cry any more. All I could think about was,

*"I don't want to be here, and it's a few days before Easter, a few days before our women day program at church, and a week before my niece's wedding."*

I just couldn't understand why. I wanted to go home. I ask the doctor to send me home for Easter. He started to send me home the next day just for Easter, but that night I started blacking out and I couldn't go home. After I started blacking out I was confined to the bed. I started crying again. I couldn't do anything for myself. I had to depend on the nurses and I didn't like that. I had an accident in my bed and it took the nurse so long to come and clean me up I started crying again. Some of the nurses were nice and some wasn't so nice. I couldn't bathe myself, and I couldn't use the bathroom. I had to lie down flat on my back to keep my pressure from going up too high. I prayed and I meditate on God's word. All I wanted to do is leave the ICU. Three died

while I was in there. I needed a nurse with me 24/7. I ask
the Lord,

*"why me? Why am I the one with the tumor? Why me,
Lord, why?"*

And God said to me,

*"why not you"*

At that moment all I could do was pray and thank  God
that I am still alive and that I found out about the tumor before
it got worse or before it was too late to do anything about it.
I know God was with me. I know He would never leave me
nor forsaken me. The devil wanted me to doubt God, so I
told the devil he is a liar. I kept my faith in Jesus because he is
my Jehovah-Rapha, a healer. Everyday I got worse I kept on
blacking out and being dizzy. I kept on praying and believing
in God. I needed the operation right away but the doctor was
scare to do it because if he did my pressure would have gone
up too high and I would have gotten a stroke, but the doctor
couldn't wait too long because if he did I could have had a
heart attack, because my pressure was high one minute and
low the next, my blood sugar was too high and my heart beat

was irregular. I had to wait another seven days before I could have the operation. I had to wait until everything was almost normal. I was taking six kind of pressure pills, three kind of sugar pills, the nurse gave a blood thinner in my stomach every morning, and I was hook up to a heart machine also taking heart pills. Most of the time I didn't know what was going on. God whisper in my ears and my mind,

*"I am still in control of your life, so don't give up. Trust in me, I will never leave you nor forsaken you."*

The devil whisper in my ears and my mind,

*"you will die on the operation table."*

I was getting very nerves, scared and depress. I couldn't figure out what was going on in my life. If I didn't have Jesus in my life I would have lost my mind. Some of the nurses were very nice to me, they did all they could to cheer me up, but nothing worked. They ordered pizza for me to eat, the devil told me the only reason why they ordered this pizza because this was my last meal and that I was going to die on the operation table. I started crying again. When my Pastor came to visit me he told me to trust God and don't give up.

One of the Evangelists from my church told me to read the 23$^{rd}$ psalms and she also told me that I would live and not die. Every chance I got I read the 23$^{rd}$ psalms. I was so scared but I didn't want my children to know it because I thought they would think that, I shouldn't be scared because I believe in Jesus and because I was saved, so I acted like I was brave. Every time I tried to get out of bed that old tumor would knock me back down and cause me to hit my head on the hard floor. I had no control of my body. That's a terrible feeling. That old tumor made me do what it wanted me to do. My hands were jerking, I tried to stop it from jerking but I couldn't stop it. I tried to stop my head from hitting the floor but I couldn't, I tried to stand up but my knees and my legs were like rubber, I had no control of them. It really made me scared just knowing that I had no control of my own body. I had so many knots on my forehead from the falls, the doctor send me to get a scan to see if I had a concussion. The last time I fell on the floor two nurses had to pick me up and took me to my bed since then I couldn't move under any circumstance. I was getting worse. I didn't know what day it was. I was always dizzy and drugged up. The devil was trying to kill me. The devil kept telling me I was going to die on the operation table. The devil told me the only reason my sister and her family from New York came to see me because I was going to die. The devil had my mind so confuse. I started crying again and all I could do was call on Jesus. If I hadn't have Jesus as my personal savior I would have given up or lost my mind. Two days before my operation the doctor told me to mark my stomach with a pen where I was suppose to be cut at. I got scared because I really didn't know where to mark my self. I thought if I mark the wrong place the doctors would have cut me there and I would have die. I didn't know what to do I didn't understand. I thought the doctors didn't know what they were suppose to do or where to cut me and that they needed me to tell them where to cut me to get the tumor. I said,

> *"Lord help me because if they need me to tell them where to cut me I don't know! Lord what am I going to do? Lord I am scared! Lord why are they asking me to mark myself! They are the doctors not me! They should know*

*where to mark me! They are the ones who are going to operate on me! Lord help me, I don't know where to mark me! Lord, suppose I tell them the wrong place to cut me! Lord should I have this operation because it looks like the doctors don't know where to cut me!"*

I didn't mark myself because I didn't know where to mark.

I started crying again and said,

*"Lord help me because I am scared. I don't know what to do!"*

My daughter was scared also. She couldn't understand why the doctors wanted me to mark myself. So she went to the nurse and ask them, why do my mother have to mark herself? The nurse told her; we just want to see if your mother is aware of what's going to happen in the operation room that's all that's for. When my daughter got through talking to the nurse she told me everything the nurse had said. I felt so much better. God helped me make the right decision by sending my daughter to get more information about the operation, because I started not to have the operation. I thought the doctors didn't know what they were doing. I thank you lord for insight. Time had come for the operation. The only thing I remember was going into the operation room and having a needle stuck in my back. After that all I remember was waking up very soar in my stomach. I lifted my grown and looked at the cut in my stomach. It scared me because the cut was so long and I had so many stitches in my stomach. I thank you Lord for a successful operation. The doctors didn't have to take my kidneys out only my adrenal glands. I lost a lot of blood so I had to have a blood transfusion. I had two units of blood put in me. I thank you Lord for guiding the doctor's hand and their mind. Ever since the operation I can bathe my self I don't need a nurse to bathe me. I can use the bathroom I don't need a bedpan. I know what day it is. I thank you Lord for giving me another chance. Lord, I thank you for not leaving me nor forsaken me. You are truly my all and all, my Jehovah-Rapha, the Lord who heals, my El-Rio, the God who sees, and my Jehovah-Jireh, the Lord who provides, and my Jehovah-Shalom, the Lord of Peace. I went to the hospital with high blood pressure, high blood sugar, irregular heartbeats, Constipation, stomach pain, weak kidneys, and a tumor. I came out the hospital with normal pressure, normal blood sugar, normal heart beats, normal bowels, no stomach pains and no tumor. God is truly a good God. I thank you Lord for every thing. I know God is able. From all the trials and tribulation I went through, I realize that my God can do all things and I can do all things through Christ, which strengthen me. I learn how to depend on Jesus. He never left me I left Him.

# BEING SINGLE, SAVED, SANCTIFIED, AND SATISFIED IN JESUS CHRIST

Being a single young lady today is not easy. There is temptation every where. In order to fight these evil spirits you have to be saved. All you have to do is confess your sins before the Lord. Confess with your mouth that Jesus is Lord and believe in your heart that God raised him from the dead and you will be saved. For it is with your heart that you believe and are justified, and it is with your mouth that you confess and are saved. The Lord shows mercy to those who loves him and keeps his commandments. God can be found

if you seek Him earnestly. God said,

> *"If my people, which are called by my name, shall humble*
> *themselves, and pray, and seek my face, and turn from*
> *their wicked ways; then will I hear from heaven, and*
> *will forgive their sins, and heal their land."*

Once you become saved then you can be sanctified. The

Lord shall establish thee a holy people unto Him, As He has

sworn unto thee, if thou shall keep the commandments of the

Lord thy God and walk in His ways. Give unto the Lord the

glory due unto his name: bring an offering, and come before

him: worship the Lord in the beauty of holiness. You must

walk not after the flesh but after the spirit. Once you become

sanctified you will be satisfied. You will have the strength to

resist the works of the flesh as long as you trust and have faith

in the Lord. Christ Jesus came into the world to save sinners.

There is no secret that we can hide from God. Yes God can

see everything. He knows everything and He is everything,

so seek the Lord and you shall live. The Lord your God is he

that goeth with you to save you. He is faithful and just to

forgive us our sins. Everyone that asketh receiveth. Repent ye, confess to God and be converted. Live unto righteousness. There is no God besides thee. You should also love yourself. A woman who does not love herself will settle for anything or anyone. You will become so thirty for love and you will rush into love blind folded without thinking. You always love too quickly, hold on too tightly, and loose too quickly the one that you have sought to embrace. You will squeeze him tightly but opens your hands to see that he has slipped through your fingers and you don't even know why he left. Then you are left alone again wondering why did he leave. If you relate well with yourself and have a strong sense of self-worth you can easily share your life with another person. You first have to love yourself before you can love another person.

In order for you to love yourself you have to feel good about yourself. Only God can make you feel good about yourself. Only God knows what you really need in life to be happy with yourself. Turn to God for happiness. Trust and believe in Him and he will give you that love you need.

You have to be aware of the works of the flesh: Adultery is a sin. Sleeping with a married man is an adultery, infidelity, degradation, and unfaithfulness. Always put yourself in the other person position,(that man's wife.) How would you feel if someone done that to you? Always do unto others, as you would have them do unto you. Always be a lady. Love yourself. Always ask this question before doing anything,

*"What would Jesus do? Would Jesus do this?"*

Exodus 20: 14 says

*"thou shall not commit adultery."*

Fornication is a sin. You should not have sex before marriage. Your body is not meant for sexual immorality, but for the Lord and the Lord for the body. By His power God raised the Lord from the dead and he will raise you also. Your body is a member of Christ himself., shall you then take the member of Christ and unite it with prostitute? No Never! Flee from sexual immorality. Your body is a temple of the Holy Spirit who is in you whom you have received from God. You are not your own. You were brought  at a price, therefore honor God with your body.

What would Jesus do? Would He fornicate? No Never!

Lasciviousness is a sin. Showing lust, tempting, and seducing are sins. You should never lust or tempt or seduce any one. Proverbs 6: 25 says

*"Do not lust in your heart after anyone."*

I peter 2: 11 says

*"dear friends, I urge you as aliens and strangers in the world, to abstain from sinful desires which war against your soul"*

Do not try to tempt, seduce or lust after a person to try and get them. Wait on the Lord. He will send someone to you who is right for you. Remember your time is not God's time. So be patient and trust in the Lord. He knows what best for you. What would Jesus do? Would he lust in His heart? No Never!

Idolatry is a sin. Worshiping Idols other gods. Exodus 20: 3-5, 23 says

*"Thou shall have no other gods before me. Thou shall*

*not make unto thee any graven image, or any likeness of any thing that is in heaven above, or that is in the earth beneath, or that is in the water under the earth: Thou shall not bow down thyself to them, nor serve them: For I the Lord thy God am a jealous God."*

You shouldn't love a man more than you love God. Do not love material things more than you love God because if you do you just made those things your idol gods; you just made that man your idol god. You should love the Lord thou God with all thy heart, with all thy soul, and with all thy mind. Hatred is a sin. Do not hate any one in your heart. Do not seek revenger or bear grude against any one

Revenge or bear a grude against anyone. How good and pleasant it is when we live together in unity. Love each other as God have loved us. Greater love has no one than this that Jesus lay down his life for us. God wants us to love everybody and not hate, or hurt, or cheat, or take revenge on each other. What would Jesus do? Would he hate you? No Never! Envy is a sin. Psalms 37: 1 says,

*"Do not fret because of evil men or be envious of those who do wrong. For they shall soon be cut down like the grass."*

The Lord's curse is on the house of the wicked, but he blesses the home of the righteous. Do not let your heart envy sinners, but always be zealous for the fear of the Lord. Love is kind, it does not envy, it does not boast, it is not proud, it is not rude, it is not self-seeking, it is not easily angered. It keeps no record of wrong. Love does not delight in evil but rejoices with the truth. Love never fails but envy does. So lets not envy one another. What would Jesus do? Would He envy? No Never! Murder is a sin. Thou shall not kill. Killing a person with a gun, knife or any other weapon is not the only way to kill a person. You could kill a person with your tongue. Yes that little red thing in your mouth can kill. Our tongue is the most powerful weapon we have. We should always try and control our tongue. Psalms 39: 1 says,

*"I will watch my ways and keep my tongue from sin*

I will put a muzzle on my mouth as long as the wicked are in my presence." He who quarrels loves sin. He whose tongue is deceitful falls into trouble. So be careful what you say to a person. Gossiping about people is killing them with your tongue. What would Jesus do? Would He gossip about a person? No Never! Drunkenness is a sin. Wine is a mocker and beer a brawler. Who ever are led astray by them is not wise. So be wise and keep your heart on the right path. Do not join those who drink too much wine and beer. When it sparkles in the cup, when it goes down smoothly in the end it bites like a snake and poisons like a viper. Your eyes will see strange things and your mind imagine confusing things. Woe to him who gives drink to his neighbors pouring it from the wineskin till they are drunk, so that they can gaze on their naked body. You will be filled with shame instead of glory. Always watch and pray that you may be able to escape all that is about to happen and that you may be able to stand before the son of man. So don't be foolish, but understand what the Lord's will is. Do not get drunk on any thing, which leads to debauchery; instead, be filled with the Holy Spirit. What would Jesus do? Would he get drunk on wine or beer? No

Never! If you do these things, which is the work of the flesh you shall not inherit the kingdom of God. You are carnal minded which is death. The flesh cannot please God. But if you are after the spirit and mind the things of the spirit you are spiritually minded which is life and peace. You should cleanse yourself from all filthiness that contaminates the body and spirit, reflecting Holiness out of reverence for God.

You should learn how to live with the fruit of the spirit in your life. You need Love because love is the duty of all to love God. You should love the Lord thy God with all our heart, with all our soul, and with all our might. You should also keep his requirements, his decrees, his laws, and his commands always. Delight yourself in the Lord and he will give you the desires of your heart. Commit your ways to the Lord, trust Him and he will do this. A person who loves God, is known by God as Christians. We all must love Jesus. Any one who love their parents or children more than God is not worthy of God. As Christians you must also love our fellowman. If you love one another God dwelled in us and His love is perfect in us. If you love God you will keep His commandments. Love is patient and love is kind it always protects, always trust, always hope, always preservers and love never fail. You need Joy. You should always rejoice before the Lord thy God in all that you do. Your heart should rejoice in the Lord. Your mouth should enlarge over your enemies. Submit to God and be at peace with Him, surely then, you will find delight in the almighty and will lift up your face to Him. God gives to a man that is good in his sight wisdom, knowledge, and Joy. You should be fill with Joy and the Holy Ghost and God is the only one who can give it to you. You need Love to have Joy.

You need peace. To have peace you have freedom from disturbance and calm. Jesus said,

> *"Peace I leave with you, my peace I give you. I do not give to you as the world gives. Do not let your heart be troubled and do not be afraid".*

Since you have been justified through faith we have peace with God through our Lord Jesus Christ, through whom you have gain access by faith into His grace in which you now stand. You must seek peace and pursue it. When you please the Lord He makes even your enemies to be at peace with you. Always love the truth and peace. God is the only one who can give you true peace. May the Lord of peace Himself give you peace always in everyway? You need Love and Joy to have Peace.

You need longsuffering (Patience). The Patient in the Spirit is better than the proud in Spirit. You shouldn't be weary in well doing, for in due season you shall reap, if you faint not. It is good that you should both hope and quietly wait for the salvation of the Lord. The trying of your faith works patience, but let patience have its work, that you may be perfect and entire, wanting nothing. Your time is not God's time so be patient and learn to trust and wait on the Lord. Remember God is always on time. You need Love, Joy, and Peace to have patience.

You need to have gentleness (kindness). Any servant of the Lord must not quarrel, instead they must be kind to everyone, able to teach, not resentful to those oppose you. You must gently instruct in the hope that God will grant you repentance leading you to a knowledge of the truth and that you will come to your sense and escape from the trap of the devil, who has taken you captive to do his will. You should be obedient and ready to do whatever is good and to slander no one but to be peaceable and considerate and to show true humility toward all people. We who are strong should bear with the failing of the weak and not to please our self. You should always please your neighbor for thier good to build them up.

You need Love, Joy, Peace, and Patience to be Gentle. You need to have goodness. When you think about the goodness of Jesus and all He has done for you your soul should cry out,

*"Hallelujah Thank God for saving me, Thank God for blessing me, Thank God for healing me."*

All you have to do is think about all the good things God has done for you. Just think about His grace and mercy, His goodness and how He gave you life. Always give God thanks thanks. Thank Him for your family, friends, food, clothes, and your home and for His son Jesus who died on the cross for your sins that you may have the right to the tree of life. You need Love, Joy, Peace, Patience, and gentleness to have Goodness.

You need Faith. Now Faith is the substance of things hope for and the evidence of things not seen. You should wait on the Lord and be of good courage and he shall strengthen your heart. In all things acknowledge the Lord and he shall direct your paths. Have faith in God. If you have faith as small as a mustard seed you can say to the mulberry tree be thou remove and it will obey you. When you are going through any situation have faith that God will bring you out or carry you around it. Be thou faithful always and God will give you a crown of life.

God will give you a crown of life. Believe and trust in God knowing that he is real even though you can't see Him.

Remember, you live by faith and not by sight. God is faithful and just and will forgive you. Things may seem like its not working out for you but have faith in God and He will work things out for you. Don't give up. Be patient and wait on the salvation of the Lord. While you are going through give God the praise inspite of and see how things work out for you. You need Love, Joy, Peace, Patient, Gentleness, and Goodness to have Faith.

You need Meekness. The Lord will guide the humble in what is right and teaches you His way. All the ways of the Lord are faithful for those who keep the demands of His covenant. Blessed are the meek for they will inherit the earth. Meekness is not being weak. A meek person is in control. They are gentle and a strong silent type person. They don't fly off the handle when being corrected. Meekness let your actions speak louder than words. You need Love, Joy, Peace, Patient, Gentleness, Goodness, and Faith to have meekness.

You need Temperance (self-control). You should have the

ability to control your actions and feelings. A person who is slow to anger is better than the mighty. You got to have the knowledge of God to have temperance. Always think before you act. You need Love, Joy, Peace, Patient, Gentleness, Goodness, Faith, Meekness to have Self-Control.

# NEEDS VS WANTS

$\mathcal{A}$ Need is something that is necessary to the fulfillment of God's plan for your life. A Desire or Want tent to be something that is not necessary but enjoyable. It can be something you wish for, hope for, or dream for. If you are walking in obedience to God you should have abundant reason to enjoy life. God wants His children to have a life overflowing with all things that are good, and certainly laughter, joy, comfort, blessing, love, health, friendship, and finance. God promises to meet all of your needs. God did not promise to meet all of your desires and wants. Philippians 4:19 says,

*"But my God shall supply all your needs according to His*

*riches in glory by Christ Jesus".*

You shouldn't turn your wants into a need and expect God to do what he said he would do in Philippians 4: 19. You might see a dress and shoe that you like and you know you don't have enough money to buy it so you use some of your rent money to buy that item. When time to pay rent you don't have enough money then you start worrying, the landlord gave you your final notice you don't know what to do then you think about Philippians 4:19. You start talking to God by saying,

*"Lord you promise to meet my needs".*

You just turn a want into a need and expect God to bail you out. It doesn't work that way. That item was a want not a need and God do not have to work things out for you. You put yourself in that mess so you get yourself out of that mess. Here's another want that you might turn into a need. You shouldn't go out looking for a man because when you do find one, you start liking him, you start having sex, you start living together, after a few months your relation isn't as great as it was. You started quarreling, calling each other names and hitting each. Then you start praying to God asking Him to fix this need for you. That need is having a man, lusting, and fornicating, these are not needs they are wants. First of all God said,

*"When a man finds a wife he finds a good thing. He didn't find you, you find him. Next, you were sinning by fornicating.*

The bible said,

*"If you can't exercise self-control let them marry. For it is better to marry, than burn".*

And another thing he wasn't in love with you, he was in lust with you, and you expect God to fix things for you. God don't have to do nothing. What are you doing for God? Are you keeping His commandments? No! Because you were fornicating, lusting, looking for a man and living together. We always want God to do things for us, but what are we doing for God? You should stop looking for a man and look to the man, Jesus Christ. Wait on the Lord and he will send you that special man. That special man can't find you because you are too busy looking. Don't be fool by these man who tell you he love you the minute he sees you. He don't love you he lust you. All he wants is sex. Open your eyes, be wise, use your brains and not your hormones. Be a lady. Love yourself. Remember God is not obligated to meet a desire or wants that you have turn into a need. God is not responsible for answering any prayer request or meet any need that does not further His plan and purpose for you on this earth. There is nothing wrong with having desires as long as it is in the confines of the purpose and will of God for your life. Sometimes we take it upon ourselves to define what is good for us. But do we really know what that is? Only God can see the beginning to the end. Only God can see the big picture of your life. Only God can look around all the corners in the road and see what is coming. Only God knows how things will turn out for us. We must rely on God's definition of good not our definition of something to be good. Only God knows fully what it means to be whole, perfect, and complete. Only God knows what is missing in your life. Suppression doesn't work in meeting your needs. Denying the need doesn't work in meeting your needs. Avoiding confrontation doesn't work in meeting your needs. Relying on another person doesn't work in meeting your needs. Striving to meet the need on your own doesn't work in meeting your needs. Only God knows how to meet your needs. You should have a spirit of total trust in and dependency upon God. Jesus gave the answer in St. Matthew 6:25-34.

> *We should turn our mind away from a preoccupation with acquiring things and focus upon God and His Kingdom.*

In other words, do not worry about your life, about what to eat or drink, or to wear or your body. Always give God thanks even when you are going through hard and difficult times. You must shift your priorities, when it comes to the things you think about, dream about and your desires. We are so concern about self, and self defined priorities and needs, that we fail to focus our heart and mind on the very things that will bring us peace and a solution for our needs. You cannot make another person love you. You cannot always have your way in everything and every situation. You cannot own everything you want to own right now. You cannot achieve anything totally in your strength and ability. You cannot do anything to absolute perfection. You cannot persuade everyone to think the way you think. Only God is absolute! He alone is omniscient (knowing everything). He alone is omnipresent (present everywhere at the same time). He alone is omnipotent (having all power). He alone governs and rules the universe according to His laws, which are unchanging. He alone is the Father who is without variation or shadow of turning. James 1:17 says,

> *"every good and perfect gift is from above, coming down from the father of the heavenly lights who does not change like shifting shadows"*

Rather than focusing on what you desires or want, which will always lead to the realization of what you can not do and be in your own strength, but turn your attention to what God have for you. Focus instead on what God can enable you to do and be. Concentrate on what He has prepared for you and desires for you. God will provide. God did not make us to go through life on our own. He made us for himself. He created you to be in fellowship with Him. When you try to get your needs met apart from God your efforts lead only to the four D's. DISAPPOINTMENTS, DISCOURAGEMENTS, DISILLUSIONMENTS, and DESPAIR. Only God can fill the empties of the human heart. Only God is sufficient to meet our deepest need for acceptance, love, and worthiness. When these are met then we can truly experience wholeness. St. John 15:4-7 says,

> *"Abide in me and I in you. I am the vine you are the branches, he who abides in me and my words abide in you, you will ask what you desire and it shall be done for you."*

To abide in Christ is to be in union with Him. Remember our desires and wants are not needs and God didn't promise to supply all our wants but He promise to supply all our needs. When ever you feel like God is far away and you can't hear from Him, don't give up. God is preparing you to be even more fruitful in the days ahead. When I felt like God isn't hearing me or seems far away, I always read St. John 15:1-4, which says,

> *"I am the true vine and my Father is the gardener. He*

*cuts off every branch in me that bears no fruit while every branch that does bear fruit He prunes so that it will be even more fruitful. You are already clean because of the word I have spoken to you. Remain in me and I will remain in you. No branch can bear fruit by it self; it must remain in the vine, neither can you bear fruit unless you remain in me".*

You should continue reading God's word, praying, and stay in contact with other believers. Once you commit your life to the Lord and give Him permission to come in and take over, He puts you in place where you grow to survive and to realize your potential. Your life would be so much easier and richer if you stop trying to create your own rain and plant your own seeds and cling instead to the true vine, which is Jesus and its only gardener who is God. Allow God to pull the weeds in your life. The sooner you let him the smaller they're be and easier to pull up. How do you use your rainy days? Do you use tough times to grow spiritual as a Christian? Do you learn from your mistake? How do you learn from hard times in your life? You should learn from your mistakes and from hard times in your life by having faith and be encourage, continue praying and trusting in the

Lord and he will hear your prayer. Do not complain about everything. Let go and let God. Treat God as the ultimate gardener. When we let God take over our self-garden, He promises you will get a bumper crop of righteousness. We know that God causes everything to work together for the good of those who love Him and are called according to His purpose for Him. Have there been moments in the past whether it was minor or major when you wished for a delete key? What made those situations so painful? What have you learned in the after math of those experiences? In what ways can you use those tough times to grow as a Christian? How can you use those tough times to help someone else? Thank God for his omniscient power and for his promise to work out all things together for good. Praise him for the way he's currently working in your life and your family life even when you sometimes don't understand the whys Remember God loves you in spite of your wrong doing, and you should love and trust Him in spite of.

# EXPERIENCING GOD'S PRESENCE IN YOUR LIFE

If you never knew what God is really like, if you have never worship in His presence, if you have never filled yourself with His words, Then how can you possibly recognize God's presence in your life. Praise God for who he is. God is the creator, he is a judge, he is your savior, he is your redeemer, and he is the Holy One and much, much more He is. He can handle any situation you have. Praise Him for what he's done in your life. Thank Him for the miracles in the bible and for His promise to care for you. Thank Him in advance for strengthening you and helping you the next time trouble strikes. You need to spend as much times as possible with the Lord. God wants you to delight yourself in him and when you do that you will be fulfilled, complete, satisfied, content, and joyful in your relationship with the Lord. Most people failed to know the Lord in a deep and satisfying way because they have a fear of God's judgment. The fear of what others might say. They lack information; they had poor teaching in the past, a failure of understanding and a lack of making the Lord the number one priority. When your relationship is one of delight in the Lord, you are not going to want to do things or use things or enter into any relationship that will damage in any way our relationship with the Lord. When you seek the Lord and delight yourself in Him.

When you delight yourself in Him you want only what is pleasing to Him and only what He wants you to have. You will be satisfied completely with what the Lord gives you, because truly your fellowship is with the Father and with His son, Jesus Christ. When God meet your inner needs with the provision of his presence, you can be assured always that part of His provision will be to give you contentment: a deep and abiding inner peace; strength: great courage and fortitude to endure all things; fulfillment: a full and satisfying feeling of supply related to your purpose on this earth. You should learn to be content regardless of your circumstance. You should be content with trouble, suffering, pain, trails, and needs. Your internal state should be content even when your outward state is trouble. The very thing that people think will bring them contentment turns out to be the very thing that creates more problems and turmoil for them. In the end only Jesus Christ can bring about contentment in our lives. Philippians 4: 13 says,

*"I can do all things through Christ which strengthens me".*

Christ not only strengthens you when you are struggling and suffering, He also strengthens you when things are going well in your life. You can learn to experience inner fulfillment as well as learn what it means to receive an abundance of external blessing. You have to know the Lord and delight in Him with increasing delight. Ask God to search your heart and look for anything that displeasing to him if you want to be set free to follow Christ fully. Ask God to break you so you can serve Him fully. Ask Him to stretch your spiritual understanding, your courage to walk with Him in a new way and ask him to lead your life down a better and a more God-focused path, you could ever lead yourself. Ask God to use you. Let Him know that you are available if He'll to do something great through you, or if He'll like to touch another person's life through you. All you have to do is be available for god to use you. Nothing can match the power of awareness that Jesus is present. The presence of a friend, a husband, a wife, your children, or anybody else can't match the presence of Jesus. We fail to look for Jesus in the midst of our storms. We fail to recognize Him when he comes. Jesus may not come to you in precisely the way you expect Him to come. He may not come to you in a form that you quickly recognize. Jesus may come to you in a totally unexpected fashion, and if you are not aware that He is present with you or that he cares enough to come to you in your storm, your response to the

Lord might be the same as that of the disciples, fear and lack of recognition. When we become aware of Jesus presence with us, several things happen to you. You immediately become comfort. When you are aware that Jesus is with you in your storm you can't help being comfort by His presence. You will be more courageous. You take courage that you can face what lies before you. You cannot help feeling more courageous when you are aware that Jesus is by your side. You will have more confident. You become confident that God will see you through. Confidence is directly related to you knowing that a current trail or time of trouble will come to an end. Who comes to you in your storm? The King of kings, The Lord of lords, The Almighty, The All Sufficient, The All Power, The All Wise, The All Loving Savior and Deliverer. With Jesus beside you who can stand against you? The devil cannot remain where Jesus dwells. The enemy cannot succeed when Jesus arrives on the scene. Your confidence is no longer in yourself to be able to survive, to endure, to conquer. Your confidence is in Jesus. No storm can drive Jesus away. No matter how fierce the storm rages or how powerful it seems to be against you. No storm should separate you from God's love. Romans 8: 15 says

> *"who shall separate us from the love of Christ? Shall tribulation, or distress, or persecution, or famine, or nakedness, or peril, or sword."*

You shouldn't let anything separate you from the love Of God because He is always there, even to the end of the age. In the form of the Holy Spirit Jesus is with you at all times. If you don't know when Jesus is present in your life just ask Him to reveal Himself to you. We usually ask the wrong questions like,

> *"Where are you Lord? Why don't you show up? Can you see what's happening to me? Or can't you see how I am struggling? Or can't you see how much pain I am in?"*

What you should be asking is,

> *"Lord, what is keeping me from seeing you? Or Lord, help me to see you and experience your presence?*

Jesus said,

> *"I am the resurrection and the life"*

When you become aware of the presence of Jesus with

you in your storm, you must become aware of Jesus is with you in the fullness of his power to be the resurrection and the life. No matter how battered, bruised, or even dead we may feel inside as the result of your struggle, Jesus is with you to raise you up into newness of life. No matter how exhausted or broken you may feel, Jesus is present with you to restore you, to heal you, and to energize you. He always comes to give life and to give life more abundantly. You should also ask Jesus to help you recognize every person He sends to help you. He not only uses a person to make you aware of His presence, He also may speak to you directly through a vision, through a message that someone preaches, or through the word of God as you read it. As you read the Bible look for Jesus to speak to you directly and intimately with a message that you know is just for you in the midst of your storm,

> *"what is Jesus doing in the passage that he bring to your mind or seems to highlight on the pages you are reading in your Bible."*

You should ask Jesus for spiritual eyes to see Him at work and spiritual ears to hear His word to you.

# MATURITY TO THE PATHWAY TO INCREASE

*M*y brethren, count it all Joy when you fall into various trails, knowing that the testing of your faith produces patience. But let patience have its perfect work, that you may be perfect and complete, lacking nothing. Humble yourself under God's mighty hand that He may lift you up in due time. Cast all your anxiety on Him because He cares for you. Be self-controlled and alert. Your enemy the devil prowls around like a roaring lion looking for someone to devour. Resist him, standing firm in the faith because you know that your brothers throughout the world are undergoing the same kind of sufferings and the God of all grace, who called you to His eternal glory in Christ after you have suffered a little while, will himself restore you and make you strong, firm and steadfast. For the Kingdom of Heaven is like a man traveling to a far country who called his own servants and delivered his goods to them. And to one He gave five talents, to another two talents, and to another one talent to each according to his own ability, and immediately he went on a journey. If you got only one talent don't bury it, use it the best you can for the up building of God's Kingdom. I Corinthians 3: 1-16 says,

> "Brother, I could not address you as spiritual but as worldly-mere infants in Christ, I gave you milk not solid food for you were not yet ready for it. Indeed you are still not ready. You are still worldly. For since there is Jealousy and quarreling among you. Are you not worldly? Are you not acting like mere men? When one says, I follow this one, and another says I follow that one, are you not mere men? We are only servants through whom you come to believe as the Lord has assigned to each his task. I planted the seed, you watered it, but God made it grow.

So neither he who plants nor he who waters is anything, but only God who makes things grow. The man who plants and the man who waters have one purpose and each will be rewarded according to his own labor. We are God's fellow workers. You are God's field; God's building, by the grace God has given you. I laid a foundation as an expert builder and someone else is building on it but each one should be careful how he builds, for no one can lay any foundation other than the one already laid which is Jesus Christ. If any man builds on this foundation using gold, silver, costly tones, woods, hay, or straw, his work will be shown for it because the day will bring it to light. It will be revealed with fire and the fire will test the quality of each man's work. If what he has built survives he will receive his reward. If it is burned up he will suffer loss; he himself will be saved but only as one escaping through the flames. Don't you know that you yourself are God's temple and that God's spirit lives in you? If anyone destroys God's temple God will destroy him. God's temple is sacred and you are that temple.

# WE NEED SPIRITUAL WISDOM

Eyes has not seen, nor ear heard, nor have entered into the heart of man the things which God has prepared for those who love Him. But God has revealed them to us through His spirit. The spirit searches all things; yes the deep things of God. What man knows the things of a man except the spirit of man, which is in Him. Even so none knows the things of God except the spirit of God. Now we have received not the spirit of the world but the spirit who is from God, that we also speak not in worlds which man's wisdom teaches but which the Holy Spirit teaches, comparing spiritual things with spiritual things. The natural man does not receive the things of the spirit of God, for they are foolishness to him, nor can he know them because they are spiritual discerned. We should always pray without ceasing. In everything give thanks; for this is the will of God in Christ Jesus for you, if you pray and believe things will happen. Remember if you pray don't worry and if you are worrying don't pray. Have peace, which is over coming your troubles in the world. You must declare the word, decide that you will believe the word, and depend on the word. You should declare something's in your life. You shouldn't operate like the world operates. The only true peace comes from Jesus. Abraham did not waver at the promise of God through unbelief but was strengthen in faith, giving glory to God and being fully convinced that what He had promise He was also able to perform. So declare the word and after you declare the word then decide to believe what you have declare in your life then start depending on it and stay in the water which is the word of God.

It is time for you to uncover; he who conceals his sins

does not prosper, but whoever confesses and renounces them finds mercy. Blessed is the man who always fears the Lord. But he who hardens his heart falls into trouble. Stop hiding sins! Stop throwing the blame on someone else! There is nothing hidden that won't be concealed. Just say,

*"here I am Lord, I need your mercy, please forgive my sins."*

Uncover your sins before God before it uncovers you. If you think you are perfect, you need to ask God to help your self-righteous soul. If you are running late to confess your sins, you can still run to God because He is holding the door open for you. Continue seeking God; Put God first in your life, read His word daily, ask the Holy Spirit to lead and guide your daily decisions like;

*"Is this something you want me to do, or have, or say? Is this right for my life?"*

Delight yourself in the Lord and always be obedience to God.

If you know lying, fornicating, stealing, adultery, etc is a sin, happy is the person if he don't do it. The wisdom of this world is always a false substitute for the wisdom of God. A person of wisdom will always be a person of mercy. (Read, I Corin. 2: 4, 13; James 3: 13-17, 5: 19-20; Galatians 6:1-2)

You should be a real soldier for God. God wants us to be real soldiers for Him. We must be strong in the grace that is in Christ Jesus. We must endure hardship like a good soldier of Christ Jesus. Remember Jesus rose from the dead, descended from David. Jesus said,

> *"This is my Gospel for which I am suffering even to the point of being chained like a criminal, but God's word is not chained, therefore I endure everything for the sake of the elect that they too may obtain the salvation that is in Christ Jesus with eternal Glory."*

If we died with Him we will also live with Him. If we endure, we will also reign with Him. If we disown Him, He will disown us. If we are faithless, He will remain faithful. For, He cannot disown Himself. We must suffer for being a Christian. We must not be surprise at the painful trail, suffering as though something strange is happening to us, but rejoice that you participate in the suffering of Christ so that we may be over joy when His glory revealed. If you are insulted because of the name of Christ, you are blessed for the spirit of glory and of God rests on you. If you suffer, it should not be as a murderer, or thief, or any kind of criminal, but suffer as a Christian. Do not be ashamed, but praise god that you bears that name. You should be quick to listen, slow to speak and slow to become angry, for man's anger does not bring about the righteousness life that God desires.

So get rid of all moral filth and the evil that is so prevalent and humble accept the word planted in you, which can save you. Do not merely listen to the word and deceive yourself but do what it says. Anyone who listen to the word but does not do what it says is like a man who looks at his face in a mirror and after looking at himself, goes away and immediately forgets what he looks like. A man who looks intently into perfect law that gives freedom and continues to do this, not forgetting what he has heard, but doing it, he will be blessed in what he does. If anyone considers himself religious and yet does not keep a tight rein on his tongue, he deceives himself and his religion is worthless. Religion that God our Father accepts as pure and faultless is this: To look after orphans and widows in their distress and to keep oneself from being polluted by the world. So let us throw off everything that hinders and the sins that so easily entangles. And let us run with perseverance the race marked out for us. Let us fix our eyes on Jesus, the author and finisher of our faith, who for the joy set before Him endured the cross scoring its shame and sat down at the right hand of the throne of God. Consider Him who endured such opposition from sinful men, so that you will not grow weary and lose heart in your struggle against sin. You have not yet resisted to the point of shedding your blood and you have forgotten that word of encouragement that addresses you as sons. Do not make light of the Lord's discipline, and do not lose heart when he rebuke you because the Lord disciplines those He loves and he punishes everyone He accepts as a sons and as a daughter. Play time is over! Pass the ball because Jesus is free! Forget all that mess and stay in the press! Walk in the resurrection power! Have a mind chance!

Receive the word of God! Let us make room for Jesus in our life. We need to put Jesus first and get right with God because we are in His plans. You need to stay connected to God and praise Him inspite of and because of and don't let anything separate you from the love of God. There is power in the name of Jesus. (Read: St. Luke 9: 57-62, 12: 18-21, 16: 22-29; St. John 6: 2-9; Acts 16:21; Romans 8: 35-39; St. Matthews 8: 27).

If you put Jesus first you will be next in line for a miracle. Have faith in God because faith will bring you out any situation. Jesus will give you rest in time of stress. Jesus said,

*"Come to me, all you who are weary and burdened and I will give you rest. Take my yoke upon you and learn of me, for I am gentle and humble in heart and you will find rest for your soul for my yoke is easy and my burden is light."*

# MY GOD IS TRULY A GOOD GOD AND HE IS ABLE TO DO ALL THINGS

*M*y God is truly a good God because I know for myself that He is Elohim, the creator.

*"In the beginning God created the heavens and the earth.*

Genesis 1:2-3 says,

*"The spirit of God was moving over the surface of the waters, then God said, " Let there be light" and there was light.*

By faith I understood that the world were prepared by the word of God. God spoke and the spirit moved. I truly believe God is El-Shaddai, the all-sufficient one. When I was in my twenties, I longed to be held in the arms of a man who would be my protector. My dear friends, how wrong I was. I wanted to be love so I began to go from man to man by doing that I became an adulteress, a whore, and a fornicator. I still felt the same when I left them, lonely and still longed to be held. I was reaching out to the wrong man. I should have been reaching out to the man (Jesus Christ). When I was in my forties my search ended on my knees, there I met my All-sufficient one, my protector, and the unconditional lover of my soul. He held me through an abusive marriage, he held me as a single parent when at times, I was overcome by loneliness, responsibilities, and the need to be held. He held me through times of great financial needs, when I felt like I have failed, when I cried at night, when I poured out my doubts about being a good mother, when I had no more strength and wonder how would I make it. He held me when I had no water in my house, everyday my daughter and I had to get water from my brother's house, from the neighbor's house and from the church. He held me from going to jail for stealing. He was there when people talked about my children and me, when jobs were taken away from me, when my car and house were taken away from me; he was there when my family and friends turn their backs on me. Through it all, my God was there for me. I can truly say He is my El-Shaddai, the All-sufficient One. I have never come away wanting. When you see God as your El-Shaddai, you can appreciate Paul's word even more

> *"Your grace is sufficient for me, for your power is perfect in weakness, most gladly, therefore, I will rather boast about my weakness that the power of Christ may dwell in me. Therefore I am well content with weakness, with insults, with distresses, with persecutions, with difficulties for Christ sakes. For when I am weak then I am strong."*

I thank everyone who talked about me because it has made me strong in the Lord.

My God is truly Jehovah-Jireh, The Lord who provides. My God has truly provided for my family and me. When I had no Job, no income, Jehovah-Jireh was there for me. He made a way out of nowhere. He never left me nor forsaken me he was there all the time. He put food on my table, clothes on our back and a roof over our head. When I had no car He gave me transportation. God is a good all the time and all the time God is good.

My God is truly Jehovah-Rapha, the Lord who heals. One day He healed my body. I had problem with my stomach, I couldn't eat, I was afraid I know I would have pain in my stomach right after I got through eating, then I would throw up, have diarrhea, and then faint. This process took one hour or more. I was afraid to eat if I wasn't at home. Most of the time I would just stay at home. One day the pain was so hard I called on Jesus He heard my cry and he healed my stomach, not only did He heal my stomach He also healed me from high blood pressure, sugar, cancer, and irregular heart beat. I can truly say He is my Jehovah-Rapha. My God is truly El-Roi, the God who sees. I was unjustly cast away.

I felt like I was unjustly cast away, I felt rejection deep inside and with rejection I had that feeling of inadequacy.

Sometimes I wonder where is God. Where is this sovereign God who promises that all things work together for the good of those who love the Lord. Does he know what is going on in my life? Does he see my pain? Many times I was mistreated, used by someone I trusted or respected. Then I tried to bury the situation, the memory of it, the emotions, the rejections because all seems too much for me to bear so I stuff it in the back of my mind, hoping it will go away but something happen and the pain comes back. I cry, I hurt and I wonder how could people be so cruel. I just couldn't take it no more, so I gave it to God. I said,

> *"Lord I can't take it any more! I need you to fix this situation! I need your help! I need you!"*

I cried to the Lord and He became my El-Roi, the God who sees. He saw my pain and He delivered me from my pain. He was there all the time when I needed Him. I believed and trusted in His name and he didn't forsake me. For the eyes of the Lord are in every place, watching the evil and the good.

# HAVE YOU EVER WONDER WHY YOUR PRAYERS HAVEN'T BEEN ANSWER?

_W_rong motive will stop your prayer from being answer. James 4:3 says,

> *"You ask and do not receive because you ask amiss that you may spend it on your pleasures."*

The things that is requested may not be wrong in God's eyes, but if the purpose is a totally self-center or tinged with evil intent, then the request is wrong and God will not respond to it. We often fail to get our needs met or prayer answer because our motivations are wrong. They are rooted in pride, self-centeredness, greed, or a desire to meet your lust. Before we ask or do anything we should ask God, if this in the will of your plan for my life.

Wrong method will stop your prayer from being answer. Some of us fail to receive God's provision for our need or fail to get our prayers answer because we reject the method that God chooses for meeting our needs; we want God to do it our way. You should be open to what God has for you. His choice will be the right one for you. God made you and He know what's best for you. So trust God and give Him a try and you won't regret it or go wrong.

Not believing (doubt) will stop your prayer from being answer. James 1:6 says,

> *"Let us ask in faith, with no doubting, for he who doubts is like a wave of the sea driven and tossed by the wind. For that person will receive anything from the Lord because he is a double-minded person, unstable in all his ways.*

We should have faith in God and do not doubt.

I John 5: 14-15 says

*" Now this is the confidence that we have in God, that if we ask anything according to His will, he hears us and if we know that He hear us, whatever we ask, we know that we have the petition that we have asked of him.*

# WOULD YOU LIKE TO KNOW JESUS PERSONALLY?

*G*od wants each of us to experience a life that has meaning, direction, love, and peace. God makes this kind of life possible through a personal relationship with his Son, Jesus Christ. Before you can accept Jesus as your Savior, here are some truths that will help us understand God's desire for you. God has a plan for your life. He appoints each person's work. God created you and has good plans for your life and to know these plans you must have a personal relationship with Jesus. God's plan gives meaning to your life. Jesus said,

*"I am the bread of life, no one who comes to me will ever be hungry again. Those who believe in me will never thirst.*

Many of us seek meaning and purpose for our life but we never find it because we look for it in the wrong people and in wrong things. When you follow God's plan for your life, the most important of which; is knowing Jesus as your Lord and Savior, you will find meaning and purpose in all that you do. God's plan gives you direction in your life. Jesus said,

*"I am the light of the world. If you follow me, you won't be stumbling through the darkness because you will have light that leads to life. Without God's direction you may not know what to do with your life. You could try a lot of things, hoping to find meaning in each one and can't find it, but if you have God in your life He will lead you and show you how to make your life count for Him and His kingdom. God's plan brings peace to your life.*

Jesus said,

*"I am leaving you with a gift; Peace of mind and heart. The peace I give isn't like the peace the world gives"*

So don't be troubled or afraid just follow Jesus as Lord and Savior and you will be filled with God's peace and you will be at peace with God. When trouble comes you will be able to have peace as you endure hardships in your life. God's plan is for you to live with Him in heaven. For God so loved the world that he gave His only son, Jesus, so that everyone who believes in him will not perish but have eternal life. Before Adam and Eve sinned they had a good relationship with God. They were able to come into God's physical presence, but after they sinned they lost that relationship and could no longer come into God's physical presence. Sin had separated them and the entire human race including you and I from God, but God did not want sin to keep his people from having a relationship with Him. So He provided a way in which we could be cleansed of our sins and live with Him in heaven forever. He gave His only son as the perfect payment for our sins.

There are some things we must do in order to know Jesus as our personal Savior. We must recognize that we are sinners. For all have sinned and for short of God's glorious stand. No one is good-not even one because we all are sinners. No one deserves eternal life with God in Heaven. No one can work hard enough to earn this life; instead, God gives eternal life to everyone who believes that Jesus Christ is His son. Before you can appreciate what Jesus had done for you, you need to recognize that you are a sinner in need of God's forgiveness. If you never acknowledge this you will never accept God's forgivingness for your sins and you will never enter into heaven. You must ask Jesus to forgive you. Now that He has brought you back as His friend, he has done this through His death on the cross in His own human body. As a result, he has brought you into the very presence of

God, and you are holy and blameless as you stand before him without a single fault. If you recognize that you are a sinner then you will be able to ask Jesus to forgive you. Do you believe that Jesus is the son of God who died on the cross for your sins, if you do and you have never thank Him for dying for you, thank Him now by saying,

> *"Lord, I thank you for paying for my sins I have committed. I give my life to you. Teach me the right way to live for you, Amen."*

You must turn away from your sins. If you were born into God's family you will not sin because God's life is in you and you will not continue sinning. Putting your faith in Jesus means that you are leaving behind your old sinful nature and that you are living to please God. You can live to please God by obeying the commands he has given us in the Bible. If you obey God you can be sure that you are a Christian and will one day have eternal life in heaven with Him.

# SOME ADVICE FOR YOU

If you are divorce or separated, give yourselves time to heal and give yourselves time to figure out what went wrong in the relationship before you rush into another one. If you don't wait you will end up doing the same thing again and that's getting a divorce or a separation. When you are in a pothole, you can't see beyond the pothole, which are your trials and tribulations and problems in our lives. You should stand still and see the salvation of the Lord. You should have faith in God. You may think your life is over when you are in that pothole but the devil is a liar. You can survive! You can make it! Because I know a man who sits high and look low, who can get you out of any situation if only you would believe and trust in Him? Some of you have a man, just to say,

*"I got a man"*

or prove that you have a man. What a wrong reason to be with a man. Every body in pants is not a real man. If that man doesn't respect or value your virginity, he doesn't love you. You need to have authority in your life. If you say,

*" I don't or need any authority in your life"*

You either don't understand authority or you are not being submissive to that authority. Everyone has someone who is in authority over you. Authority gives direction for what you should do. Some of us won't take it because we think we know the best way or the short cut, or we think we know everything and we end up in trouble or problems. If only you would listen to the voice of authority things would be so much better in your life. Some of you are so stress out because you don't want any one to tell you anything. The minute the voice of authority tells you something, your flesh rises up and you start fussing. You must be submissive to the authority of God (His Word). If you are not submissive to His word you don't respect God's word. If you don't understand authority remember understanding comes after submitting. To keep God in your life you need to spend time with God, trust in Him and not yourself. Keep away from idols, which are things or people that you spend more time with than you spend with God.

If you are a Christian, and all of a sudden you become a sinner by focusing on the work of the flesh, it is because you stop spending time with God, you stop seeking God and you stop putting God first in your life.

When I was a sinner, I was digging a well with no water in it and I was still thirsty, running from man to man. I thought these men could quench my thirst. Oh how wrong I was! In St.John 4:13, Jesus said,

> *"whoso ever drinketh of this water shall thirst again, but whoso ever drinketh of the water that I shall give shall never thirst and the water that I shall give him shall be in him a well of water springing up into everlasting."*

Never put yourself in a situation where you can't get yourself out. But if you let God put you there He will always get you out. Never dig a well with any water in it. The word of God is medicine for your flesh. Always rejoice in the Lord. Let your gentleness be evidence to all. The Lord is near. Do not be anxious about anything but in everything by prayer and petition with thanksgiving. Present your request to God He will hear you. And the peace of God, which transcends all understanding, will guard your heart and mind in Christ Jesus. When you get God's peace you will have a new heart and a new spirit (a new thinking). When God put a seed in your life, you need wisdom, understanding and insight to produce it, so ask God to give you these things. Remember there are time and a season for everything, so be patient and wait on God

We shouldn't operate in our wants but always in our needs. We need to make some sacrifices in our life. We need to script something's off in our life, things that we don't need.

Never have a fear of rejection in your heart. If you do you will do anything so you won't be rejected. Some of you will be abuse before you be rejected. Some of you will give your body to any man before you are rejected because you are afraid he won't love you or he will leave you if you don't have sex with them. If a man tells you,

*"it's over or I don't want to see you any more because you won't have sex with him",*

tell him good-bye! If he can't respect you he doesn't love you and he isn't good enough for you.

Some people are afraid of being rejected by their children, they let their children do anything they want, and they won't even discipline them, because they are afraid their child won't love them. So what if your children tell you they don't love you, they don't mean it; they just said that because they couldn't get their way. God called you to be their parent not their best friend. Take control of your life and say,

*"I will not compromise to be accepted because I know a man who will accept me just as I am and His name is Jesus.*

Never let the fear of rejection push you to compromise. Don't compromise your standards to be accepted. You can't let your feelings or emotions rule over your life. Remember, you have authority over your life so don't let your feelings rule your life because if you do it will move you out of the will of God. Don't let the works of the flesh rule your life. If something feels good is not necessary right for you. Fornication feels good but it's wrong, revenge feels good but it's wrong. Stop trying to protect your feelings, and ignoring your future, by not, protecting your future. Always take control of the situation with the fruit of the spirit. Emotion will take you back to bondage and you will end up in the forty years wilderness. God is a right now God. God is not one of our sources, He is our only source and what we thought was our source is God's resource for us. The earth is the Lord's and all it's fullness. Be free. Stop letting your feelings control you. Let the hurt go. Move on with your life. Start walking into your authority. Let go and let God. The devil likes to suggest. Every time he suggest, cast it down. Cast your burdens on the Lord and he shall sustain you.

When God speaks to your heart don't send it to your head but send it to your feet and walk into it. Cast all your cares unto the Lord. Obey the Lord when you are in the will of God. Stay focus, believe, obey, and commit. Always say, I will not let anything separate me from the love of God. Remember the devil will always attack us when our blessings are on the tail of a thing.

Sometimes God takes us through the wilderness to humble us, to test us and to know or learn what's in our heart. Remember our wilderness is only our training ground, so hold on, don't give up and you will be able to hold out to your promise land. Don't die in the wilderness. Keep a cool head and a warm heart because you are very bless and you can pass that test. Remember the answer is not in a man but the man, Jesus. Your God shall supply all your needs according to His riches in glory by Christ Jesus so cast all your cares upon Him for He cares for you. May the Lord of peace Himself give you peace always in everyway?

# SUMMARY

$\mathcal{O}$f you are confuse and searching for the right direction
try the man, Jesus, not a man. I tried Jesus and He made
everything all right. He gave me love, joy, peace, happiness,
long-suffering, gentleness, goodness, faith, meekness, and
self-control. He also gave me a peace of mind and the Holy
Ghost and the Holy Ghost gave me direction. I had to first
seek the kingdom of God and He added all those other things.
I tried a man for direction but it didn't work. Jesus is the
answer for the world today. I am not telling you to leave your
husband, boyfriend or your man, but I am telling you to get
the man before you get a man and God will send the right

man to you. Ask God to give you the Holy Ghost because it will guide you in the right direction. It is good that you should hope and wait quietly for the salvation of the Lord. Wait patiently for the Lord and he will have favor in you and he will hear your cry. God is love and he loves, you. As you travel the road to victory you will have some trails and some tribulations, and you will have some bad days and you will have some good days. So when you travel your journey go to believers blvd, keep going through the green light turn on the bridge of faith, keep straight don't turn on doubt lane, don't start doubting your prayers because it hasn't been answer yet. Keep straight, oh my! There is lying lane, please don't turn there; the devil is lying to you when he says your prayers will never be answer. Remember you are on the bridge of faith and prayer changes thing. So keep straight, but look there is stealing lane, don't turn there; you don't have to steal money to get what you want all you have to do is pay your tithes and offering and God will give you one hundred fold. Keep straight, and don't turn because fornication lane is only one mile down on the right and lust lane is on the left. I know that man look good and you would like to sleep with him but don't turn, keep straight and go three miles down one for the father, one for the Son and one for the Holy ghost. Keep going to grace blvd, God will give you grace if only you believe. Keep going till you get to prayer blvd but remember gossip lane is on the left don't turn there, I know it's hard not to gossip about that sister you saw with the deacon last night, but keep straight and yield not to temptation, because adultery lane is one block down, don't turn, call on Jesus and keep straight to the blvd of the fruit of the spirit. Love blvd, you should love one another just like Jesus love us. Keep straight to gentleness blvd, always be kind to everyone. There is goodness blvd, just think about the goodness of Jesus and all he has done for you. Don't turn on envy lane, because it's the next block, I know you are wondering how that sister got that expensive outfit and she doesn't work and you work hard every day and can't afford to buy something like that, please don't turn just keep straight to temperance blvd and ask God to give you self-control, keep going to joy blvd, remember God will give you joy in hard times, keep straight to peace blvd, God will give you a peace of mind be careful not to turn on hatred lane, you are now thinking about that person who done you wrong, talked bad about you, lied on you and slept with your husband, don't worry just keep straight to meekness blvd, remember God will guide the humble in what is right, God said revenge is His. Keep straight to long-suffering blvd because you have to go through something's in our life, so keep straight to faith blvd. Have faith in God and He will make everything alright. Keep straight to Victory Blvd, you got the victory because you didn't turn. Give God the praise because you made it to Victory Blvd.BELIEVE...

BECAUCE EMMANUEL LIVES

I EXPECT VICTORY EVERYTIME